STORYBOOK MAZES

by
Dave Phillips

Dover Publications, Inc.
New York

Published in Canada by General Publishing
Company, Ltd., 30 Lesmill Road, Don Mills,
Toronto, Ontario.
Published in the United Kingdom by Constable
and Company, Ltd., 10 Orange Street, London
WC2H 7EG.

Storybook Mazes is a new work, first published
by Dover Publications, Inc., in 1978.

International Standard Book Number:
0-486-23628-5
Library of Congress Catalog Card Number:
77-93195

Manufactured in the United States of America
Dover Publications, Inc.
180 Varick Street
New York, N.Y. 10014

Introduction

Everyone likes a good story and everyone likes solving twisting, turning mazes. So Dave Phillips has combined many of your favorite stories with mazes of his own invention. Now you can actually share the adventures with the characters. You will be able to rescue Maid Marian along with Robin Hood and his band, to slay the fierce Minotaur with Theseus and to follow the yellow brick road with Dorothy and her strange friends. There are 23 stories in all and every one has its own maze. At the end of each story the instructions for the maze are given in **boldface**. The solutions are also included. They start on page 48. They show the shortest route for solving the mazes, but other solutions are possible.

The stories have been adapted for the mazes. They have been shortened and a few of the details have been changed. So, while these maze stories are great fun, they are not meant to replace the thrill of reading the originals.

Many good editions are available of the works of Lewis Carroll, Carlo Collodi, Washington Irving, Mark Twain, Robert Louis Stevenson and Jules Verne. The fairy tales of Charles Perrault have been wonderfully illustrated by Gustave Doré (Dover 22311-6). *The Wonderful Wizard of Oz* is available in a facsimile of the original, with illustrations by W. W. Denslow (Dover 20691-2). Traditional English stories are retold by Joseph Jacobs in *English Fairy Tales* (Dover 21818-X). *Household Stories* (Dover 21080-4), by the Brothers Grimm, contains many of their most popular tales. Howard Pyle's version of the exploits of the inhabitants of Sherwood Forest, *The Merry Adventures of Robin Hood* (Dover 22043-5), has itself become a classic. For a retelling of the Greek myths, Thomas Bulfinch's *The Age of Fable* is perhaps the version most frequently read. *The Arabian Nights Entertainments* (Dover 22289-6), edited by Andrew Lang, contains many of the best tales from the original.

Contents

Cinderella

Many years ago there was an orphan named Ella who lived with her cruel stepmother and two ugly stepsisters in a faraway kingdom. They were so jealous of Ella's beauty that they forced her to do all the daily chores and to wait on them hand and foot. While they dressed in the richest clothing and lived in luxury, Ella had to wear rags and sleep among the cinders in the kitchen. Because of this she became known as Cinderella. One day the stepmother received an invitation to a grand ball that was to be given at the palace in honor of Prince Charming. The Prince had decided that the time had come to marry, so all the unwed maidens of the kingdom were to attend. When Cinderella asked if she could go, her stepmother laughed at her.

On the night of the ball the stepmother and stepsisters went off in their finery, leaving Cinderella alone and weeping. Suddenly Cinderella's fairy godmother appeared and told her to dry her tears, for she *would* go to the ball. With a wave of her magic wand she turned Cinderella's rags into a gorgeous gown and a pumpkin and some mice into a golden coach with footmen. Most wondrous of all, on Cinderella's feet was a gleaming pair of dancing slippers made entirely of glass. Cinderella thanked her fairy godmother, but as she drove off she was warned to return before midnight, for when the clock finished striking twelve the enchantment would end, and all would be as it had been before.

The ball was already underway when Cinderella arrived. The Prince had been unable to find any maiden he liked. But as soon as he saw Cinderella he fell in love with her and the two danced together for hours. Cinderella was enjoying herself so much that she forgot the time. Suddenly the clock began to strike twelve. Remembering the fairy godmother's warning, she tore herself from the startled Prince's arms and fled from the ballroom into her coach, which thundered off. In her haste a glass slipper fell from her foot. The Prince found it and vowed to tour the kingdom, searching for the maiden whose foot fit the slipper. She would become his bride.

Help Prince Charming find his way to Cinderella, but stay clear of the wicked stepmother and ugly stepsisters.

start

end

3

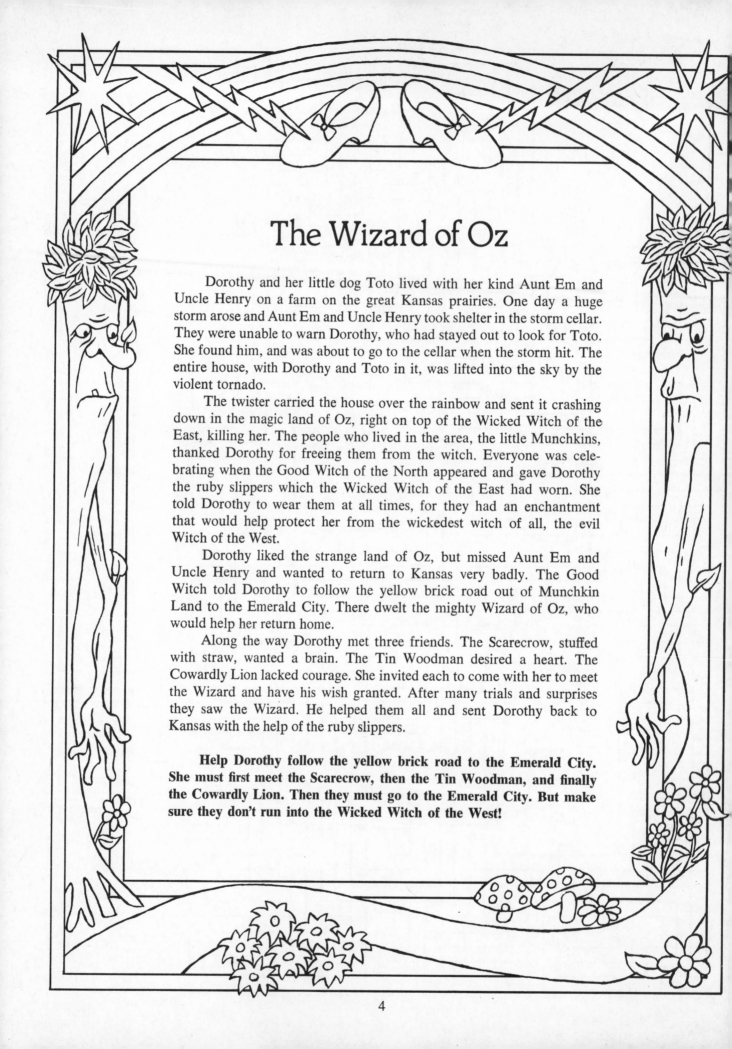

The Wizard of Oz

Dorothy and her little dog Toto lived with her kind Aunt Em and Uncle Henry on a farm on the great Kansas prairies. One day a huge storm arose and Aunt Em and Uncle Henry took shelter in the storm cellar. They were unable to warn Dorothy, who had stayed out to look for Toto. She found him, and was about to go to the cellar when the storm hit. The entire house, with Dorothy and Toto in it, was lifted into the sky by the violent tornado.

The twister carried the house over the rainbow and sent it crashing down in the magic land of Oz, right on top of the Wicked Witch of the East, killing her. The people who lived in the area, the little Munchkins, thanked Dorothy for freeing them from the witch. Everyone was celebrating when the Good Witch of the North appeared and gave Dorothy the ruby slippers which the Wicked Witch of the East had worn. She told Dorothy to wear them at all times, for they had an enchantment that would help protect her from the wickedest witch of all, the evil Witch of the West.

Dorothy liked the strange land of Oz, but missed Aunt Em and Uncle Henry and wanted to return to Kansas very badly. The Good Witch told Dorothy to follow the yellow brick road out of Munchkin Land to the Emerald City. There dwelt the mighty Wizard of Oz, who would help her return home.

Along the way Dorothy met three friends. The Scarecrow, stuffed with straw, wanted a brain. The Tin Woodman desired a heart. The Cowardly Lion lacked courage. She invited each to come with her to meet the Wizard and have his wish granted. After many trials and surprises they saw the Wizard. He helped them all and sent Dorothy back to Kansas with the help of the ruby slippers.

Help Dorothy follow the yellow brick road to the Emerald City. She must first meet the Scarecrow, then the Tin Woodman, and finally the Cowardly Lion. Then they must go to the Emerald City. But make sure they don't run into the Wicked Witch of the West!

end

start

5

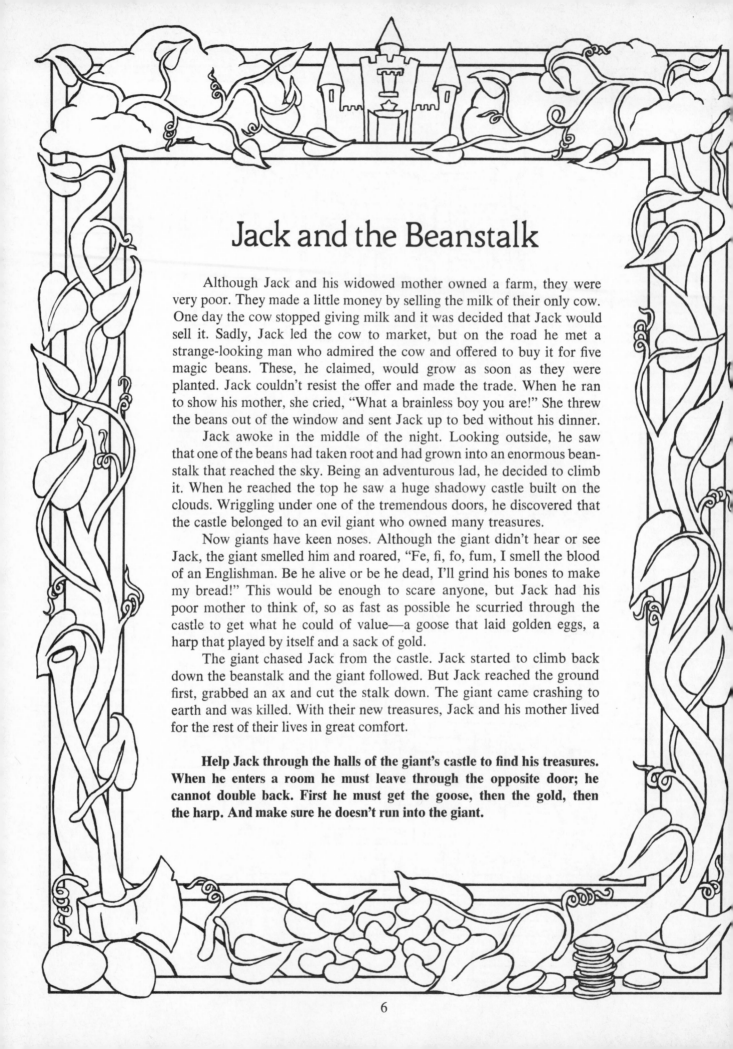

Jack and the Beanstalk

Although Jack and his widowed mother owned a farm, they were very poor. They made a little money by selling the milk of their only cow. One day the cow stopped giving milk and it was decided that Jack would sell it. Sadly, Jack led the cow to market, but on the road he met a strange-looking man who admired the cow and offered to buy it for five magic beans. These, he claimed, would grow as soon as they were planted. Jack couldn't resist the offer and made the trade. When he ran to show his mother, she cried, "What a brainless boy you are!" She threw the beans out of the window and sent Jack up to bed without his dinner.

Jack awoke in the middle of the night. Looking outside, he saw that one of the beans had taken root and had grown into an enormous beanstalk that reached the sky. Being an adventurous lad, he decided to climb it. When he reached the top he saw a huge shadowy castle built on the clouds. Wriggling under one of the tremendous doors, he discovered that the castle belonged to an evil giant who owned many treasures.

Now giants have keen noses. Although the giant didn't hear or see Jack, the giant smelled him and roared, "Fe, fi, fo, fum, I smell the blood of an Englishman. Be he alive or be he dead, I'll grind his bones to make my bread!" This would be enough to scare anyone, but Jack had his poor mother to think of, so as fast as possible he scurried through the castle to get what he could of value—a goose that laid golden eggs, a harp that played by itself and a sack of gold.

The giant chased Jack from the castle. Jack started to climb back down the beanstalk and the giant followed. But Jack reached the ground first, grabbed an ax and cut the stalk down. The giant came crashing to earth and was killed. With their new treasures, Jack and his mother lived for the rest of their lives in great comfort.

Help Jack through the halls of the giant's castle to find his treasures. When he enters a room he must leave through the opposite door; he cannot double back. First he must get the goose, then the gold, then the harp. And make sure he doesn't run into the giant.

end

start

7

Snow White

Snow White was a princess. Her mother died when Snow White was a baby. Her father, the King, remarried after a few years. Although Snow White's stepmother was very beautiful, she was also very wicked and a sorceress. She would stand for hours in front of her enchanted mirror, admiring her reflection and asking, "Mirror, mirror on the wall, who is the fairest of us all?" The mirror always replied, "You are fairest of them all." But one day, when Snow White had grown, it replied, "Queen, you are full fair, 'tis true, but Snow White fairer is than you."

The Queen went into a rage and ordered one of the royal huntsmen to take the princess into the forest and slay her. The huntsman's heart, however, was touched by Snow White's innocence and beauty, so he let her escape. Snow White ran deep into the forest, stopping in front of a little cottage. Seven dwarfs who mined gold from a nearby mountain lived there. They heard Snow White's tale and offered her a home with them. Soon all eight were leading a happy life together.

But one day the wicked Queen went before her mirror and asked her usual question. The answer chilled her—"Queen, thou art of beauty rare, but Snow White living in the glen, with the seven little men, is a thousand times more fair." Realizing that she had been fooled, the Queen poisoned an apple and went in disguise to the house of the seven dwarfs. She gave the apple to Snow White, who ate it and fell as though dead. The dwarfs placed her in a glass coffin in the woods. But Snow White was not dead. She was under an enchantment that could only be broken by a prince's kiss. One day a prince, having heard of Snow White, was riding through the forest. The Queen tried desperately to keep him from Snow White.

The prince must find Snow White to awaken her with his kiss. But first he must destroy the evil Queen, avoiding the deadly bolts of enchantment. Approach her from the path that ends at her head. Once she is dead, proceed from the path that starts at her feet and continue until Snow White is reached.

end

start

9

Alice's Adventures in Wonderland

One warm summer afternoon, while making daisy chains as she sat on the riverbank, Alice was surprised to see a rabbit run past her. Not any rabbit, but one wearing a coat and vest, who looked at his pocket watch and squealed in alarm because he found he was late for an appointment. Alice followed him and tumbled into his rabbit hole. Although she fell for a long distance she landed at the bottom with a gentle bump.

Nearby was a table on which stood a bottle and a small box. The bottle had a label that read "drink me." The box contained a little cake with the words "eat me" on it. Alice tasted both. The drink made her shrink and the cake made her so tall that her head reached the ceiling. She was so upset that she wept buckets, then found herself shrinking again. Before she knew it, she was swimming in a pool of her own tears, along with a very unhappy and nervous mouse.

She floated right into Wonderland, where she met the most unusual creatures. There was the blue caterpillar who smoked a hookah. The Cheshire Cat could appear and disappear at will, leaving only his grin visible. The melancholy Mock Turtle had some of the features of a turtle and some of a calf. There was the Queen of Hearts, who loved to play croquet using flamingos as mallets and hedgehogs as balls. The irritable monarch ordered people beheaded for the least offense. After many strange adventures, Alice awoke on the riverbank to find that it had all been a dream.

See Alice through Wonderland, leading her to the mad tea party given by the March Hare, Mad Hatter and the Dormouse at the lower right, but keep her clear of the Queen of Hearts and her playing-card soldiers.

start

end

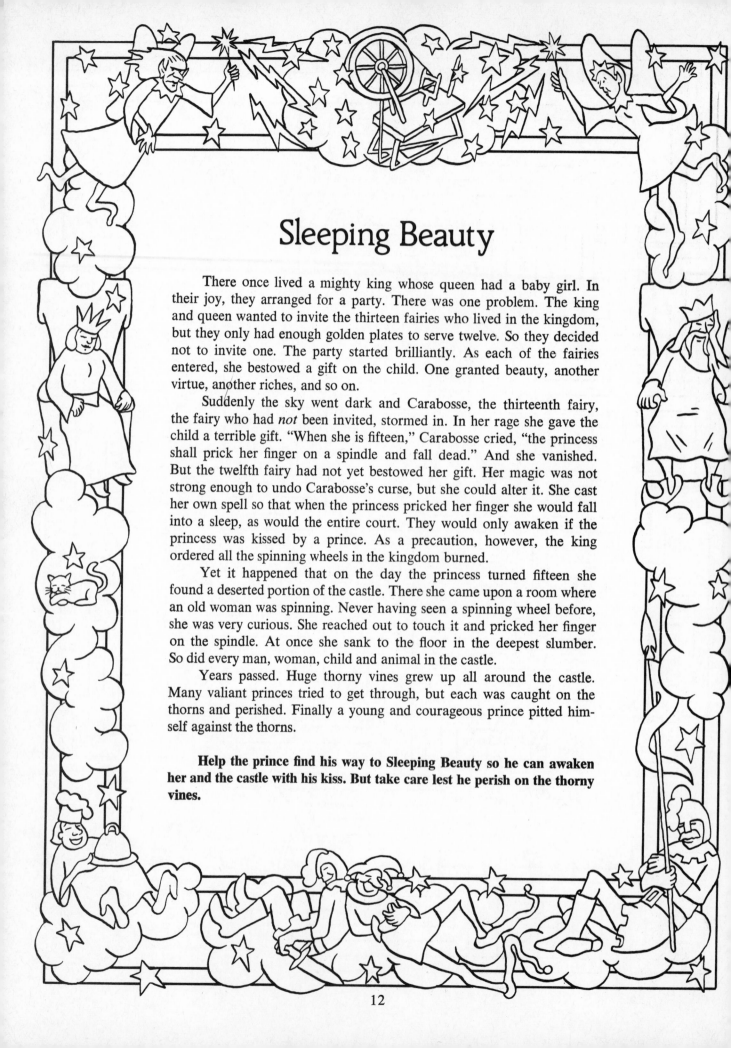

Sleeping Beauty

There once lived a mighty king whose queen had a baby girl. In their joy, they arranged for a party. There was one problem. The king and queen wanted to invite the thirteen fairies who lived in the kingdom, but they only had enough golden plates to serve twelve. So they decided not to invite one. The party started brilliantly. As each of the fairies entered, she bestowed a gift on the child. One granted beauty, another virtue, another riches, and so on.

Suddenly the sky went dark and Carabosse, the thirteenth fairy, the fairy who had *not* been invited, stormed in. In her rage she gave the child a terrible gift. "When she is fifteen," Carabosse cried, "the princess shall prick her finger on a spindle and fall dead." And she vanished. But the twelfth fairy had not yet bestowed her gift. Her magic was not strong enough to undo Carabosse's curse, but she could alter it. She cast her own spell so that when the princess pricked her finger she would fall into a sleep, as would the entire court. They would only awaken if the princess was kissed by a prince. As a precaution, however, the king ordered all the spinning wheels in the kingdom burned.

Yet it happened that on the day the princess turned fifteen she found a deserted portion of the castle. There she came upon a room where an old woman was spinning. Never having seen a spinning wheel before, she was very curious. She reached out to touch it and pricked her finger on the spindle. At once she sank to the floor in the deepest slumber. So did every man, woman, child and animal in the castle.

Years passed. Huge thorny vines grew up all around the castle. Many valiant princes tried to get through, but each was caught on the thorns and perished. Finally a young and courageous prince pitted himself against the thorns.

Help the prince find his way to Sleeping Beauty so he can awaken her and the castle with his kiss. But take care lest he perish on the thorny vines.

end

start

13

Little Tom Thumb

A poor woodcutter and his wife had seven sons. One of the sons was no bigger than your thumb, so they named him Tom Thumb. Although Tom did not grow over the years, he was very bright. One day the woodcutter told his wife they were so poor that they could no longer feed their sons. This was very upsetting to her. She said she could not bear to see her sons starve. The woodcutter said he would take them into the Black Forest and lose them so they would be eaten by wolves. The woodcutter did not want to do this, but he saw no other choice.

Now Tom Thumb had heard this and immediately thought of a plan to save himself and his brothers. He filled his pockets with small white pebbles. When his father led them through the forest, Tom dropped the pebbles one at a time along the way. The woodcutter left his sons deep in the forest and sadly went home. The brothers were afraid, but Tom told them he had left a trail of pebbles which they could follow back home. The boys arrived home before dark, much to the surprise of the woodcutter and his wife.

The woodcutter decided to take his sons into the Black Forest again. Tom did not have time to fill his pockets with pebbles but, much to his relief, his mother gave to each of her sons a loaf of bread, thinking it to be their last meal. The woodcutter took his sons back into the forest, deeper and farther than before. Along the way Tom dropped crumbs of bread to mark the trail. To his dismay, Tom found that the birds of the forest had eaten all the crumbs, and when his father left them, they were truly lost. But Tom was brave and managed to guide his brothers out of the forest. When they arrived home again, they found that their father had come into a fortune and he swore that he would never lead them into the Black Forest again.

Starting in the center, help Tom lead his brothers out of the Black Forest, staying away from the wolves. If you are as clever as Tom, you can do it.

start

end

15

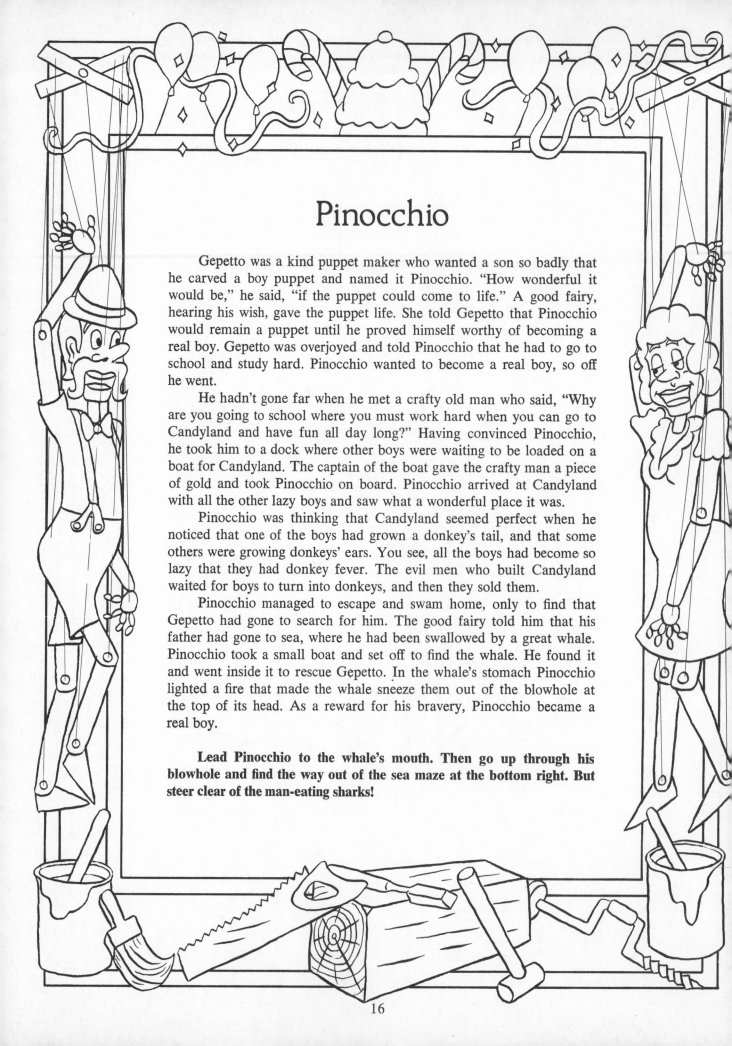

Pinocchio

Gepetto was a kind puppet maker who wanted a son so badly that he carved a boy puppet and named it Pinocchio. "How wonderful it would be," he said, "if the puppet could come to life." A good fairy, hearing his wish, gave the puppet life. She told Gepetto that Pinocchio would remain a puppet until he proved himself worthy of becoming a real boy. Gepetto was overjoyed and told Pinocchio that he had to go to school and study hard. Pinocchio wanted to become a real boy, so off he went.

He hadn't gone far when he met a crafty old man who said, "Why are you going to school where you must work hard when you can go to Candyland and have fun all day long?" Having convinced Pinocchio, he took him to a dock where other boys were waiting to be loaded on a boat for Candyland. The captain of the boat gave the crafty man a piece of gold and took Pinocchio on board. Pinocchio arrived at Candyland with all the other lazy boys and saw what a wonderful place it was.

Pinocchio was thinking that Candyland seemed perfect when he noticed that one of the boys had grown a donkey's tail, and that some others were growing donkeys' ears. You see, all the boys had become so lazy that they had donkey fever. The evil men who built Candyland waited for boys to turn into donkeys, and then they sold them.

Pinocchio managed to escape and swam home, only to find that Gepetto had gone to search for him. The good fairy told him that his father had gone to sea, where he had been swallowed by a great whale. Pinocchio took a small boat and set off to find the whale. He found it and went inside it to rescue Gepetto. In the whale's stomach Pinocchio lighted a fire that made the whale sneeze them out of the blowhole at the top of its head. As a reward for his bravery, Pinocchio became a real boy.

Lead Pinocchio to the whale's mouth. Then go up through his blowhole and find the way out of the sea maze at the bottom right. But steer clear of the man-eating sharks!

start

end

17

The Pied Piper of Hamelin

Hamelin was a lovely town. There was but one thing wrong: the town was infested with rats. They were brazen, and felt no fear of man. Rats overran the houses by the thousands, spilling out into the streets. At night sleep was almost impossible; the noise made by the scurrying of countless rats was deafening.

The townspeople tried everything they could think of to rid themselves of the rats. Nothing worked. No one knew what to do. One day a curious fellow came to town. He was lanky, with bells on his boots and a feather in his hat. With him he carried a flute. He introduced himself to the Mayor of Hamelin as the Pied Piper, and claimed that he could destroy the hated rats. The mayor promised him his weight in gold if he succeeded, thinking the man had little chance where so many others had failed.

The Piper accepted and immediately went out into the streets. He played his flute and danced merrily through the town. Everyone laughed and thought him a fool. But some noticed that a few of the rats had begun to follow him. Then their number grew. Rats bounded out of sewers, they came streaming from the doorways, they dropped from the eaves. And they all joined in line, following the Piper, hopping, jumping and squeaking, completely entranced by his music. He led the rats to a river near Hamelin where they all drowned.

When he returned to the town, he was amazed to find that the Mayor went back on his word, and denied him the promised gold. The Piper once again began to play his flute. Only this time the children of Hamelin, every last boy and girl, followed the Piper. The merry line of skipping and singing children followed him out of Hamelin. None of them was ever seen or heard from again.

See if you can help the Pied Piper gather the rats, one after another. When you enter a box containing a rat, you must leave through the opposite path. You may not double back. Then leave the town at the bottom right.

start

end

The Legend of Sleepy Hollow

Ichabod Crane was a schoolmaster in the Hudson Valley in the days just after the American Revolution. He was a highly educated man, but for some reason he believed in ghosts. Although he was tall and thin and looked a bit like a scarecrow, he was popular with the ladies. Ichabod fancied Katrina Van Tassel, daughter of a wealthy farmer, and courted her with great style and elegance. The lady, however, was also courted by brawny Brom Bones. The two became fierce rivals, and Brom threatened that he would take care of Ichabod, although he didn't say how.

Late on Halloween night Ichabod was returning from a party. Entering Sleepy Hollow he became extremely nervous, for he remembered the legend about the place. It was said that the hollow was haunted by the ghost of a Hessian soldier whose head had been knocked off by a cannonball during the Revolution. Trotting along briskly on his horse, Ichabod whistled to keep his spirits up, for he imagined he could see ghostly shapes among the bare branches of the trees peering at him with pale eyes.

He quickened the pace of his horse, turned a bend in the road and saw the shape of a figure atop a huge black horse looming in the distance. To his horror, he realized that no head sat atop the horseman's shoulders but that, in its stead, he carried a jack-o'-lantern under one arm. Suddenly the horseman gave chase. Terror-stricken, Ichabod made a mad dash for the stone bridge which led to the old church. There he thought he would find safety.

The next day Ichabod was missing. The townspeople searched for him and found his horse at the church and bits of a smashed jack-o'-lantern, but they never saw Ichabod again. Some say that the Headless Horseman managed to carry him off, others that Brom Bones had dressed as the Horseman to scare Ichabod away from Katrina. What do you think?

Guide Ichabod and his quaking horse out of the hollow, across the stone bridge and to the church without encountering any of the specters, especially the Headless Horseman.

end

start

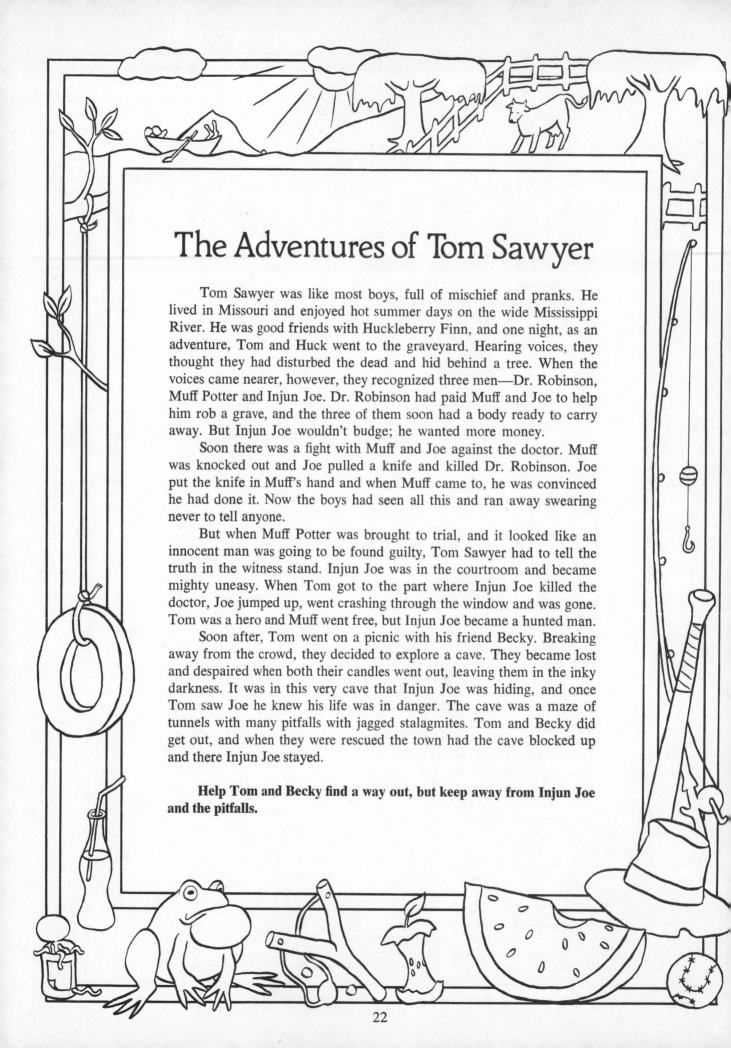

The Adventures of Tom Sawyer

Tom Sawyer was like most boys, full of mischief and pranks. He lived in Missouri and enjoyed hot summer days on the wide Mississippi River. He was good friends with Huckleberry Finn, and one night, as an adventure, Tom and Huck went to the graveyard. Hearing voices, they thought they had disturbed the dead and hid behind a tree. When the voices came nearer, however, they recognized three men—Dr. Robinson, Muff Potter and Injun Joe. Dr. Robinson had paid Muff and Joe to help him rob a grave, and the three of them soon had a body ready to carry away. But Injun Joe wouldn't budge; he wanted more money.

Soon there was a fight with Muff and Joe against the doctor. Muff was knocked out and Joe pulled a knife and killed Dr. Robinson. Joe put the knife in Muff's hand and when Muff came to, he was convinced he had done it. Now the boys had seen all this and ran away swearing never to tell anyone.

But when Muff Potter was brought to trial, and it looked like an innocent man was going to be found guilty, Tom Sawyer had to tell the truth in the witness stand. Injun Joe was in the courtroom and became mighty uneasy. When Tom got to the part where Injun Joe killed the doctor, Joe jumped up, went crashing through the window and was gone. Tom was a hero and Muff went free, but Injun Joe became a hunted man.

Soon after, Tom went on a picnic with his friend Becky. Breaking away from the crowd, they decided to explore a cave. They became lost and despaired when both their candles went out, leaving them in the inky darkness. It was in this very cave that Injun Joe was hiding, and once Tom saw Joe he knew his life was in danger. The cave was a maze of tunnels with many pitfalls with jagged stalagmites. Tom and Becky did get out, and when they were rescued the town had the cave blocked up and there Injun Joe stayed.

Help Tom and Becky find a way out, but keep away from Injun Joe and the pitfalls.

start

end

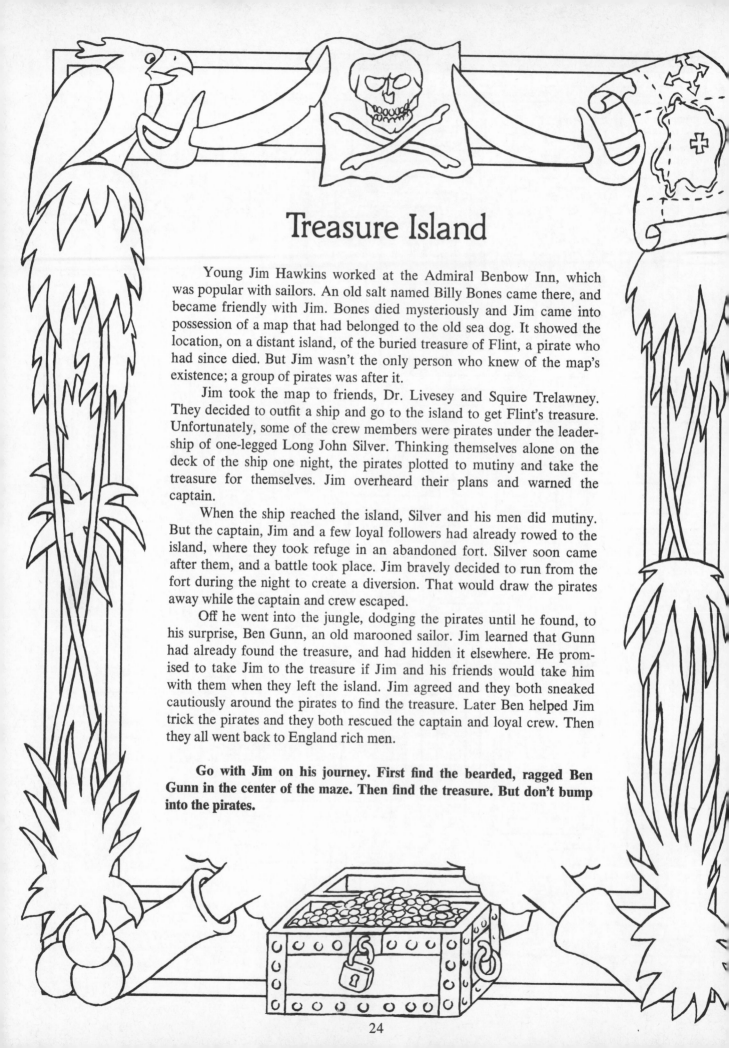

Treasure Island

Young Jim Hawkins worked at the Admiral Benbow Inn, which was popular with sailors. An old salt named Billy Bones came there, and became friendly with Jim. Bones died mysteriously and Jim came into possession of a map that had belonged to the old sea dog. It showed the location, on a distant island, of the buried treasure of Flint, a pirate who had since died. But Jim wasn't the only person who knew of the map's existence; a group of pirates was after it.

Jim took the map to friends, Dr. Livesey and Squire Trelawney. They decided to outfit a ship and go to the island to get Flint's treasure. Unfortunately, some of the crew members were pirates under the leadership of one-legged Long John Silver. Thinking themselves alone on the deck of the ship one night, the pirates plotted to mutiny and take the treasure for themselves. Jim overheard their plans and warned the captain.

When the ship reached the island, Silver and his men did mutiny. But the captain, Jim and a few loyal followers had already rowed to the island, where they took refuge in an abandoned fort. Silver soon came after them, and a battle took place. Jim bravely decided to run from the fort during the night to create a diversion. That would draw the pirates away while the captain and crew escaped.

Off he went into the jungle, dodging the pirates until he found, to his surprise, Ben Gunn, an old marooned sailor. Jim learned that Gunn had already found the treasure, and had hidden it elsewhere. He promised to take Jim to the treasure if Jim and his friends would take him with them when they left the island. Jim agreed and they both sneaked cautiously around the pirates to find the treasure. Later Ben helped Jim trick the pirates and they both rescued the captain and loyal crew. Then they all went back to England rich men.

Go with Jim on his journey. First find the bearded, ragged Ben Gunn in the center of the maze. Then find the treasure. But don't bump into the pirates.

start

end

25

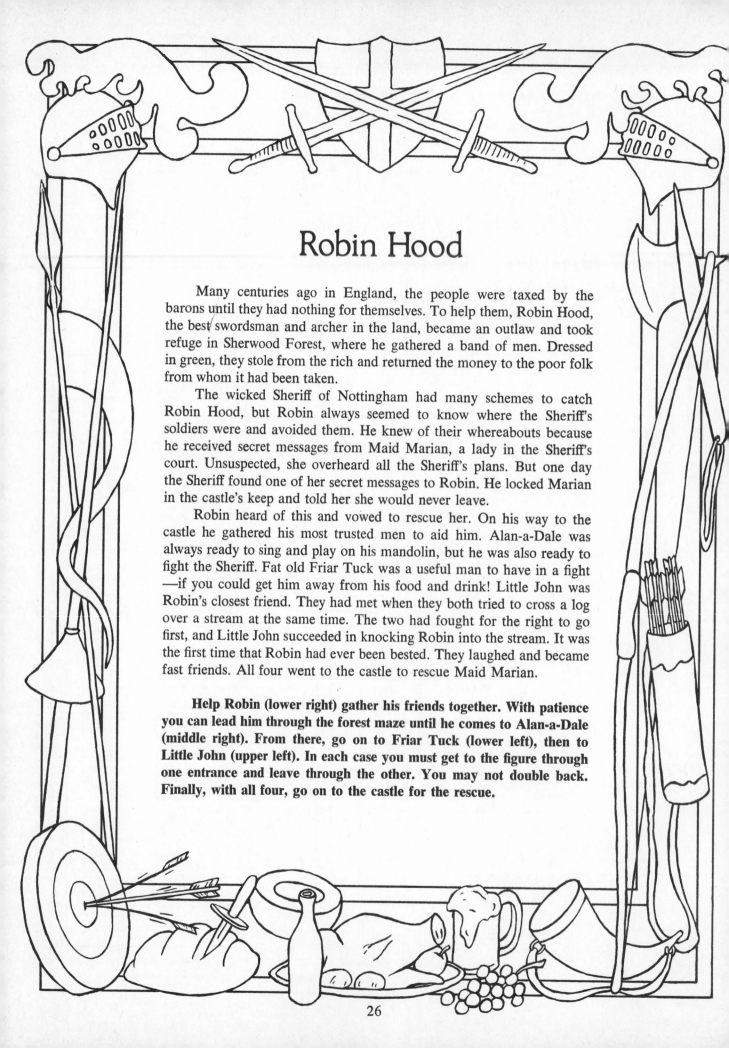

Robin Hood

Many centuries ago in England, the people were taxed by the barons until they had nothing for themselves. To help them, Robin Hood, the best swordsman and archer in the land, became an outlaw and took refuge in Sherwood Forest, where he gathered a band of men. Dressed in green, they stole from the rich and returned the money to the poor folk from whom it had been taken.

The wicked Sheriff of Nottingham had many schemes to catch Robin Hood, but Robin always seemed to know where the Sheriff's soldiers were and avoided them. He knew of their whereabouts because he received secret messages from Maid Marian, a lady in the Sheriff's court. Unsuspected, she overheard all the Sheriff's plans. But one day the Sheriff found one of her secret messages to Robin. He locked Marian in the castle's keep and told her she would never leave.

Robin heard of this and vowed to rescue her. On his way to the castle he gathered his most trusted men to aid him. Alan-a-Dale was always ready to sing and play on his mandolin, but he was also ready to fight the Sheriff. Fat old Friar Tuck was a useful man to have in a fight —if you could get him away from his food and drink! Little John was Robin's closest friend. They had met when they both tried to cross a log over a stream at the same time. The two had fought for the right to go first, and Little John succeeded in knocking Robin into the stream. It was the first time that Robin had ever been bested. They laughed and became fast friends. All four went to the castle to rescue Maid Marian.

Help Robin (lower right) gather his friends together. With patience you can lead him through the forest maze until he comes to Alan-a-Dale (middle right). From there, go on to Friar Tuck (lower left), then to Little John (upper left). In each case you must get to the figure through one entrance and leave through the other. You may not double back. Finally, with all four, go on to the castle for the rescue.

end

start

27

Daniel Boone

Daniel Boone was a restless man. Shunning the comforts of a settled life, he braved the hardships of the wilderness to open new frontiers. As a scout, Daniel was brave and swift and could shoot and track with the best mountain men. Along with thirty men he was hired to cut a trail 300 miles through the wilderness to the Kentucky River. At the end of the trail they built a fort and log cabins and named the settlement Boonesborough in honor of Daniel.

Daniel led many pioneers along the Wilderness Road to the rich lands of the West. He was married to Rebeccah Bryan, and they had two fine sons and a lovely daughter. One day his daughter was in a canoe with two friends when they were captured by Indians. Daniel took a hunting party with him and, using his amazing tracking skills, found the Indians and rescued his daughter and her friends.

On another occasion, Daniel himself was captured by the fierce Shawnee tribe. Blackfish, the Shawnee chief, saw how brave Daniel was and adopted him as his son. Blackfish refused to let Daniel leave the camp, but Daniel was set on going. One night he overheard the chief and his warriors making plans to attack Boonesborough. While they were busy with a war dance, Daniel made his escape. As soon as Blackfish discovered that Daniel was gone, he sent his finest braves after him. But Daniel was cunning as a fox. He made it to the fort, having traveled 160 miles in four days—on foot! He warned Boonesborough, and the fort, ready for the attack, defeated the Shawnees.

Help Daniel to escape from the Indian camp and find his way to the fort at Boonesborough at the upper right. Be stealthy and avoid being captured by the Indians.

29

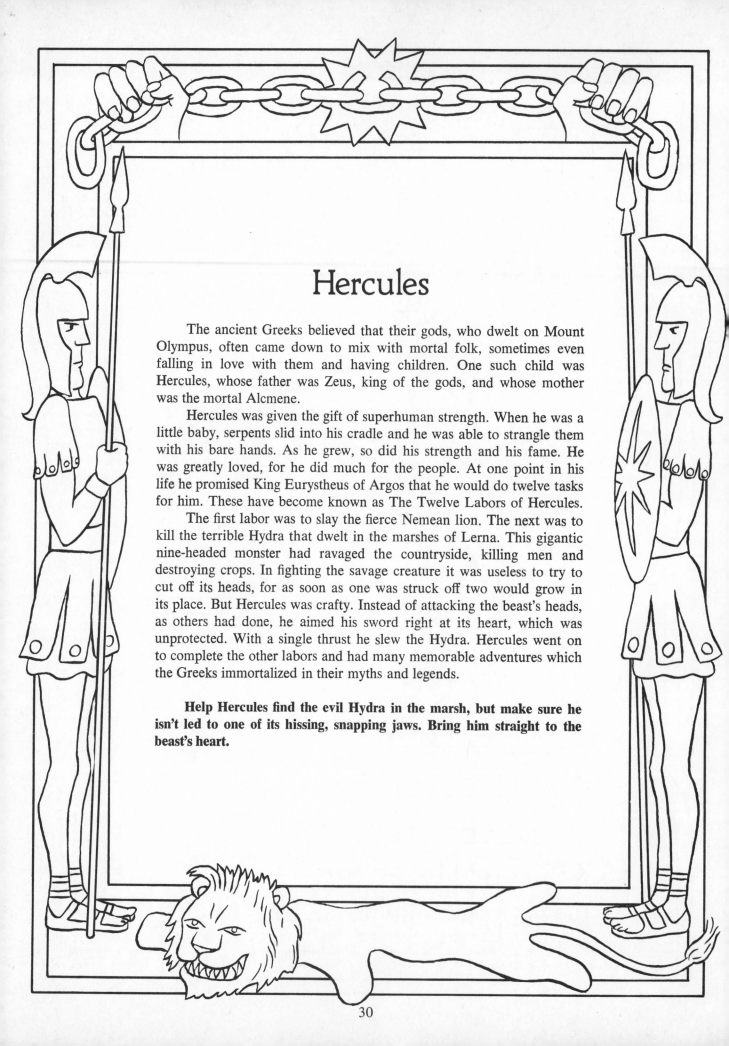

Hercules

The ancient Greeks believed that their gods, who dwelt on Mount Olympus, often came down to mix with mortal folk, sometimes even falling in love with them and having children. One such child was Hercules, whose father was Zeus, king of the gods, and whose mother was the mortal Alcmene.

Hercules was given the gift of superhuman strength. When he was a little baby, serpents slid into his cradle and he was able to strangle them with his bare hands. As he grew, so did his strength and his fame. He was greatly loved, for he did much for the people. At one point in his life he promised King Eurystheus of Argos that he would do twelve tasks for him. These have become known as The Twelve Labors of Hercules.

The first labor was to slay the fierce Nemean lion. The next was to kill the terrible Hydra that dwelt in the marshes of Lerna. This gigantic nine-headed monster had ravaged the countryside, killing men and destroying crops. In fighting the savage creature it was useless to try to cut off its heads, for as soon as one was struck off two would grow in its place. But Hercules was crafty. Instead of attacking the beast's heads, as others had done, he aimed his sword right at its heart, which was unprotected. With a single thrust he slew the Hydra. Hercules went on to complete the other labors and had many memorable adventures which the Greeks immortalized in their myths and legends.

Help Hercules find the evil Hydra in the marsh, but make sure he isn't led to one of its hissing, snapping jaws. Bring him straight to the beast's heart.

start

end

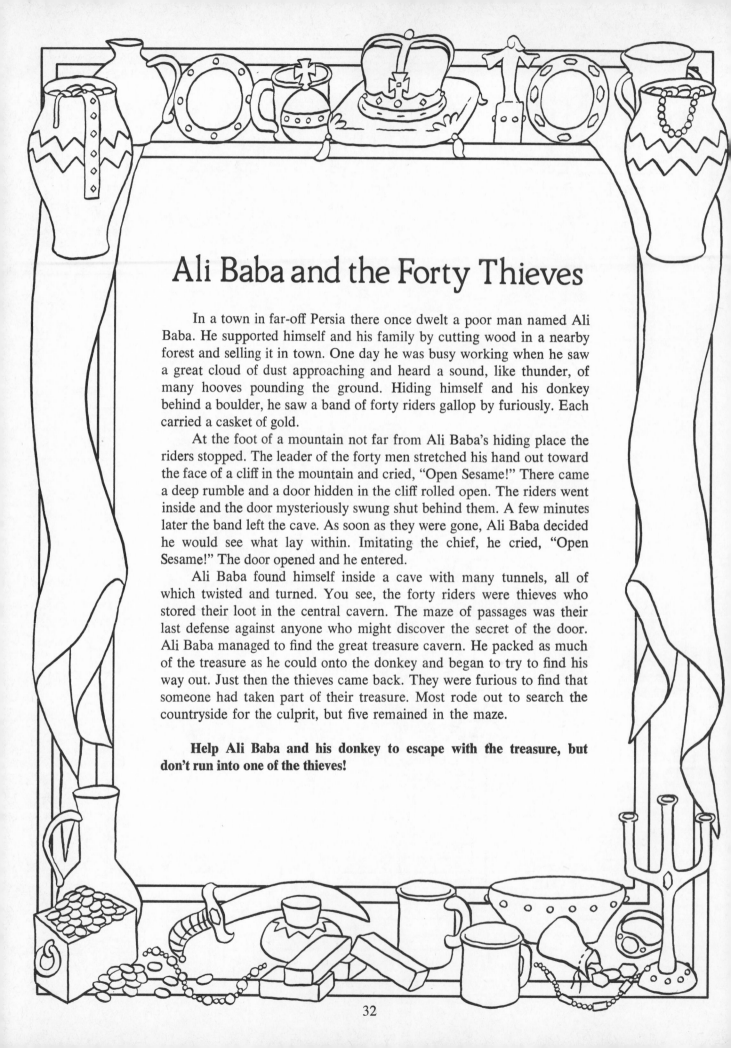

Ali Baba and the Forty Thieves

In a town in far-off Persia there once dwelt a poor man named Ali Baba. He supported himself and his family by cutting wood in a nearby forest and selling it in town. One day he was busy working when he saw a great cloud of dust approaching and heard a sound, like thunder, of many hooves pounding the ground. Hiding himself and his donkey behind a boulder, he saw a band of forty riders gallop by furiously. Each carried a casket of gold.

At the foot of a mountain not far from Ali Baba's hiding place the riders stopped. The leader of the forty men stretched his hand out toward the face of a cliff in the mountain and cried, "Open Sesame!" There came a deep rumble and a door hidden in the cliff rolled open. The riders went inside and the door mysteriously swung shut behind them. A few minutes later the band left the cave. As soon as they were gone, Ali Baba decided he would see what lay within. Imitating the chief, he cried, "Open Sesame!" The door opened and he entered.

Ali Baba found himself inside a cave with many tunnels, all of which twisted and turned. You see, the forty riders were thieves who stored their loot in the central cavern. The maze of passages was their last defense against anyone who might discover the secret of the door. Ali Baba managed to find the great treasure cavern. He packed as much of the treasure as he could onto the donkey and began to try to find his way out. Just then the thieves came back. They were furious to find that someone had taken part of their treasure. Most rode out to search the countryside for the culprit, but five remained in the maze.

Help Ali Baba and his donkey to escape with the treasure, but don't run into one of the thieves!

end

start

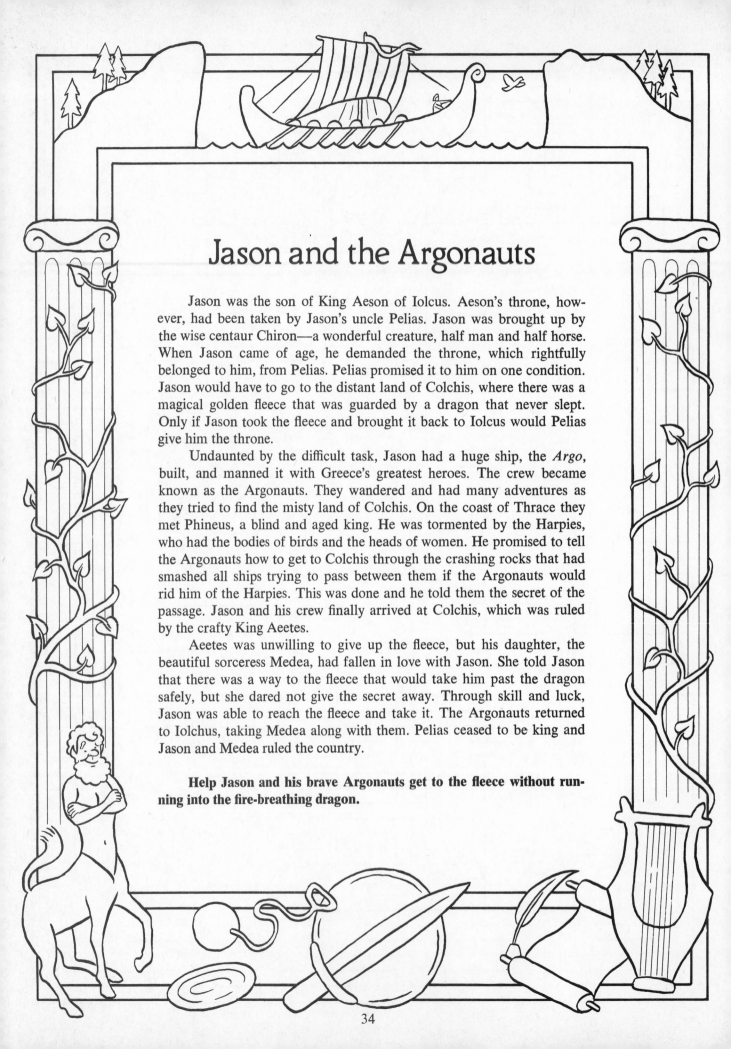

Jason and the Argonauts

Jason was the son of King Aeson of Iolcus. Aeson's throne, however, had been taken by Jason's uncle Pelias. Jason was brought up by the wise centaur Chiron—a wonderful creature, half man and half horse. When Jason came of age, he demanded the throne, which rightfully belonged to him, from Pelias. Pelias promised it to him on one condition. Jason would have to go to the distant land of Colchis, where there was a magical golden fleece that was guarded by a dragon that never slept. Only if Jason took the fleece and brought it back to Iolcus would Pelias give him the throne.

Undaunted by the difficult task, Jason had a huge ship, the *Argo*, built, and manned it with Greece's greatest heroes. The crew became known as the Argonauts. They wandered and had many adventures as they tried to find the misty land of Colchis. On the coast of Thrace they met Phineus, a blind and aged king. He was tormented by the Harpies, who had the bodies of birds and the heads of women. He promised to tell the Argonauts how to get to Colchis through the crashing rocks that had smashed all ships trying to pass between them if the Argonauts would rid him of the Harpies. This was done and he told them the secret of the passage. Jason and his crew finally arrived at Colchis, which was ruled by the crafty King Aeetes.

Aeetes was unwilling to give up the fleece, but his daughter, the beautiful sorceress Medea, had fallen in love with Jason. She told Jason that there was a way to the fleece that would take him past the dragon safely, but she dared not give the secret away. Through skill and luck, Jason was able to reach the fleece and take it. The Argonauts returned to Iolchus, taking Medea along with them. Pelias ceased to be king and Jason and Medea ruled the country.

Help Jason and his brave Argonauts get to the fleece without running into the fire-breathing dragon.

end

start

35

Aladdin and the Magic Lamp

Aladdin was the son of a poor Chinese tailor. He was hopelessly lazy. One afternoon a mysterious stranger came up to him—an African magician who thought Aladdin would fit into a scheme he had. In flattering words he told Aladdin that he needed a swift and clever boy to help him uncover a great treasure. Aladdin agreed to help. The magician led Aladdin far into the mountains. They came to a stone slab in the earth. "Lift the stone," said the magician, "and you will find a passageway that leads through a maze to the treasure. You may take as many of the precious gems as you want. There is but one thing I must have, and that is the lamp that stands atop a pillar."

As soon as he entered the mountain, Aladdin realized why the magician had not gone to get the lamp himself. The tunnels were filled with poisonous snakes whose bite was certain death! How clever the magician thought he was. If Aladdin should perish, he could always find another boy to fetch the lamp, at no danger to himself. Aladdin found the lamp. He returned to the entrance of the cave, but refused to give the lamp to the magician until he was outside. Enraged, the magician shut the slab, leaving Aladdin sealed inside.

At first Aladdin despaired, but then he began to think. Why did the magician want the old lamp, which seemed of little value? Looking at the lamp, Aladdin rubbed it to remove some dust. Suddenly, with a blinding flash, a spirit appeared. He was the genie of the lamp who appeared when the lamp was rubbed. It was his task to grant every wish of the lamp's owner. Aladdin was quick to use his new power. He had the genie take him from the cave, build a lavish palace for him, and fill it with priceless treasures. The evil magician was punished and Aladdin married a sultan's daughter.

Help Aladdin find the lamp. Make sure that he stays away from the snakes.

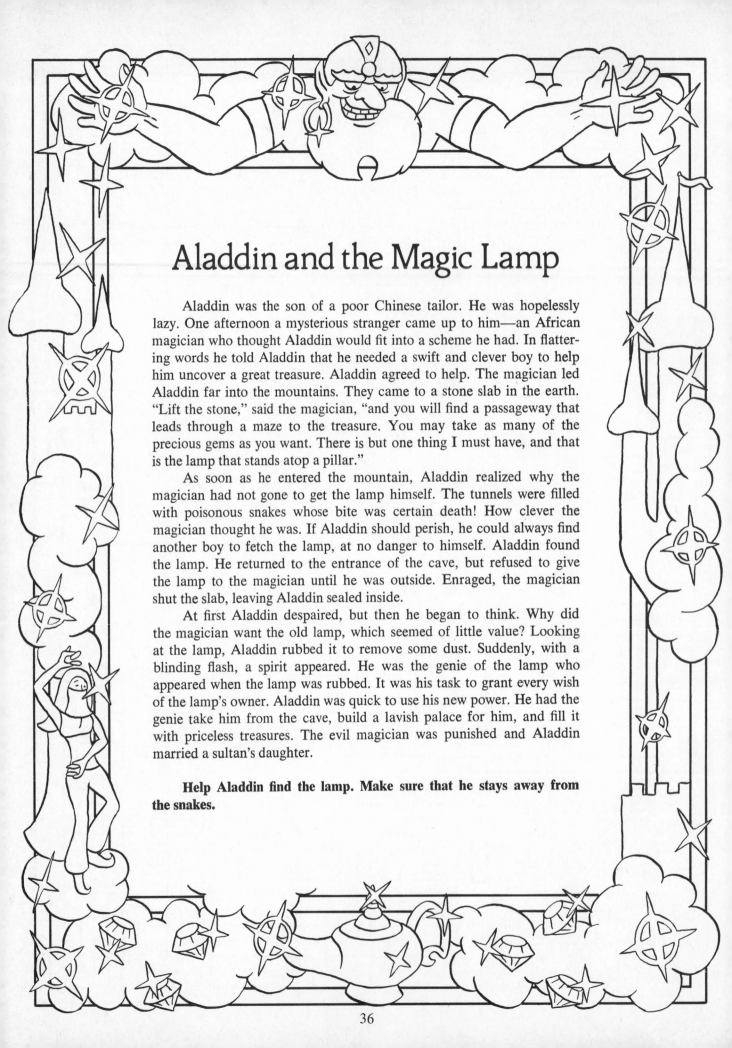

start

end

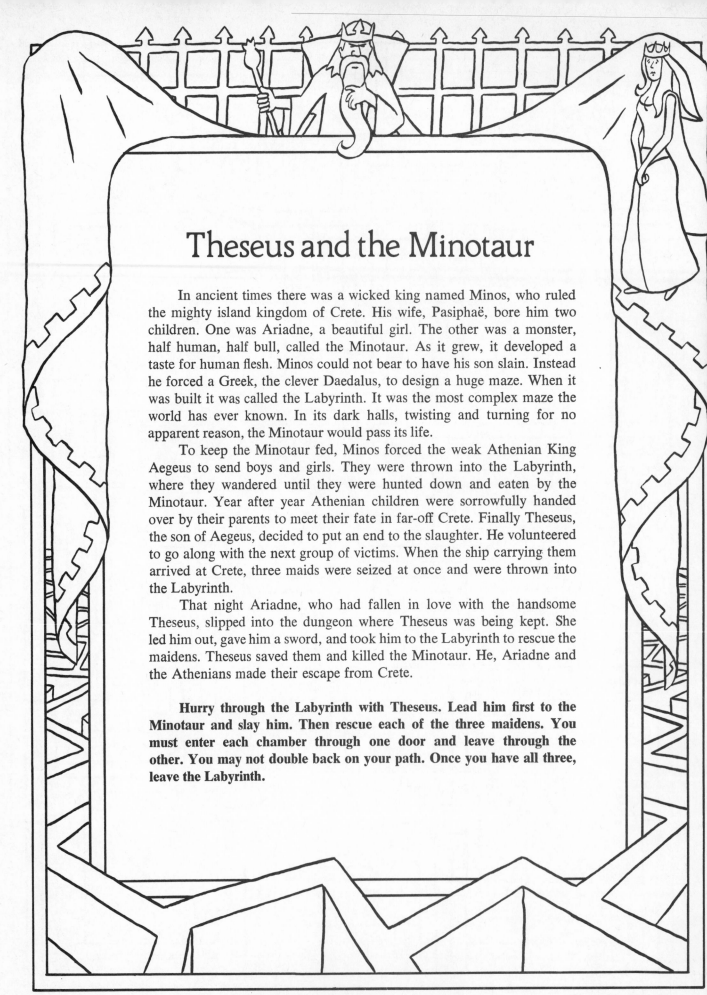

Theseus and the Minotaur

In ancient times there was a wicked king named Minos, who ruled the mighty island kingdom of Crete. His wife, Pasiphaë, bore him two children. One was Ariadne, a beautiful girl. The other was a monster, half human, half bull, called the Minotaur. As it grew, it developed a taste for human flesh. Minos could not bear to have his son slain. Instead he forced a Greek, the clever Daedalus, to design a huge maze. When it was built it was called the Labyrinth. It was the most complex maze the world has ever known. In its dark halls, twisting and turning for no apparent reason, the Minotaur would pass its life.

To keep the Minotaur fed, Minos forced the weak Athenian King Aegeus to send boys and girls. They were thrown into the Labyrinth, where they wandered until they were hunted down and eaten by the Minotaur. Year after year Athenian children were sorrowfully handed over by their parents to meet their fate in far-off Crete. Finally Theseus, the son of Aegeus, decided to put an end to the slaughter. He volunteered to go along with the next group of victims. When the ship carrying them arrived at Crete, three maids were seized at once and were thrown into the Labyrinth.

That night Ariadne, who had fallen in love with the handsome Theseus, slipped into the dungeon where Theseus was being kept. She led him out, gave him a sword, and took him to the Labyrinth to rescue the maidens. Theseus saved them and killed the Minotaur. He, Ariadne and the Athenians made their escape from Crete.

Hurry through the Labyrinth with Theseus. Lead him first to the Minotaur and slay him. Then rescue each of the three maidens. You must enter each chamber through one door and leave through the other. You may not double back on your path. Once you have all three, leave the Labyrinth.

start or end

start
or end

39

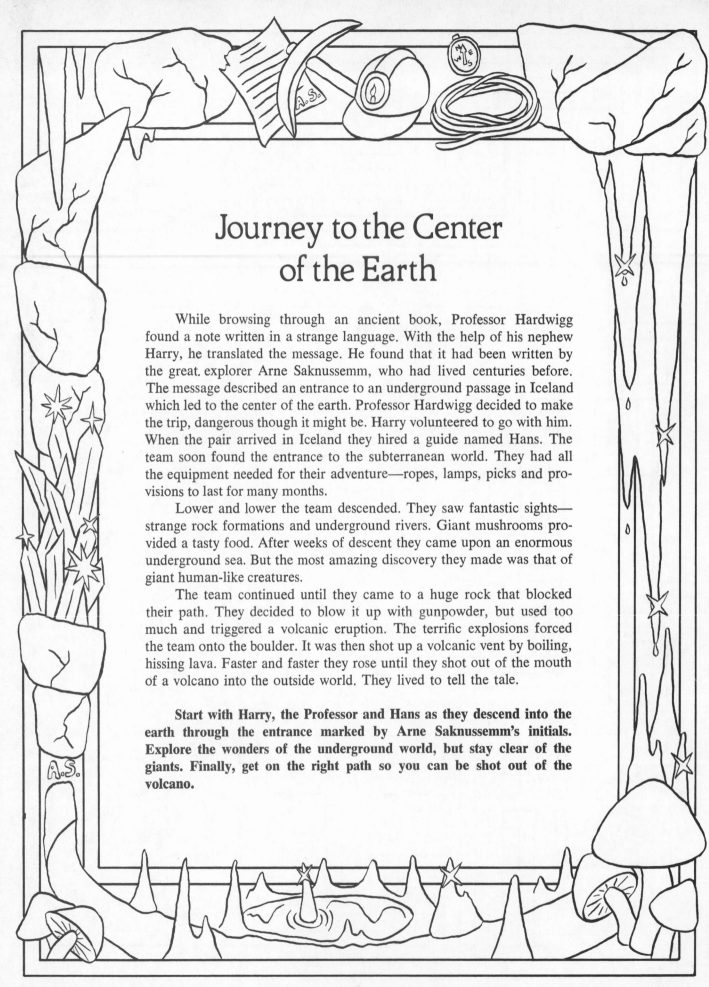

Journey to the Center of the Earth

While browsing through an ancient book, Professor Hardwigg found a note written in a strange language. With the help of his nephew Harry, he translated the message. He found that it had been written by the great explorer Arne Saknussemm, who had lived centuries before. The message described an entrance to an underground passage in Iceland which led to the center of the earth. Professor Hardwigg decided to make the trip, dangerous though it might be. Harry volunteered to go with him. When the pair arrived in Iceland they hired a guide named Hans. The team soon found the entrance to the subterranean world. They had all the equipment needed for their adventure—ropes, lamps, picks and provisions to last for many months.

Lower and lower the team descended. They saw fantastic sights—strange rock formations and underground rivers. Giant mushrooms provided a tasty food. After weeks of descent they came upon an enormous underground sea. But the most amazing discovery they made was that of giant human-like creatures.

The team continued until they came to a huge rock that blocked their path. They decided to blow it up with gunpowder, but used too much and triggered a volcanic eruption. The terrific explosions forced the team onto the boulder. It was then shot up a volcanic vent by boiling, hissing lava. Faster and faster they rose until they shot out of the mouth of a volcano into the outside world. They lived to tell the tale.

Start with Harry, the Professor and Hans as they descend into the earth through the entrance marked by Arne Saknussemm's initials. Explore the wonders of the underground world, but stay clear of the giants. Finally, get on the right path so you can be shot out of the volcano.

41

From the Earth to the Moon

The Gun Club met in Baltimore, Maryland, during the last century. It discussed and developed better ways of shooting missiles from guns. During times of war the club was busiest. Now, however, there were no wars in the world, and little chance of one. One day Impey Barbicane, the president of the club, sent a message to all the members. He announced that he had thought of a project that would put their talents to work again. Barbicane wanted the club to invent a cannon to shoot a missile to the moon! The members were thrilled and started work.

Soon the enormous cannon was built. It was sunk into the ground with just the muzzle projecting. The necessary calculations were made to aim it for the moonshot. All that remained was to design the projectile they would use. Just then Michel Arden, a Frenchman, wrote to Barbicane. He said that if the projectile were made hollow, he would be willing to journey inside it to the moon. Barbicane decided that he, Arden and another member of the club, Captain Nichol, would journey to the moon together.

When the missile was built, it was equipped with life supports. It also had rockets to enable it to make the return journey to the Earth. Finally, the cannon was fired and the missile was shot to the moon. When the crew arrived, they found the moon inhabited by strange insect-like creatures. The moon beings took the three Earthlings to their leader. He told them they would be held prisoners for the rest of their lives!

Help the three brave men escape from the center and reach their projectile so they can return to Earth safely. Take great care that they stay clear of the moon men.

43

Twenty Thousand Leagues Under the Sea

In 1867 it was reported that a sea monster was sinking ships of war. Riding a ship of the U.S. Navy was a Frenchman, P. Aronnax, his servant, Conseil, and the harpooner, Ned Land. The ship was attacked by the monster and sunk. Aronnax, Conseil and Land managed to swim to the back of the monster and found that it was made of iron! It was, in fact, a submarine! Members of the crew took the three down to meet the man who had designed the vessel, the mysterious Captain Nemo.

Nemo told them that he hated the greed and evil of mankind. Most of all, he hated war and the suffering it caused. To try to wipe out war, his ship, the *Nautilus*, traveled the seas, sinking all ships of war. Nemo did not mind that the warships carried innocent men aboard. Aronnax, Conseil and Land were astonished by the luxury on the *Nautilus*. The Captain let the three men know they could roam the ship freely, but that he would never allow them to return to the outside world.

As they toured the oceans of the world they saw and experienced many remarkable things. Nemo had discovered underground rivers which allowed him to take the ship deep into the hearts of the continents. They went to the South Pole. One of their most exciting adventures was a visit to the ruins of a sunken city in the lost continent of Atlantis. Eventually the ship was caught in a giant whirlpool and was destroyed. Although Aronnax managed to escape, few people believed the tale he told.

Travel on the "Nautilus" to the sunken city. Enter the city from the bottom entrance and leave it from the left side. Take the ship back out of the maze. Steer clear of the wiggling tentacles of the octopuses and squids.

start

end

45

Around the World in Eighty Days

Mr. Phileas Fogg, who lived in London, was always on time. His whole life was run according to a strict timetable. Like many wealthy Englishmen, he belonged to en exclusive gentlemen's club. One day, he and his fellow members discussed a recent daring robbery. The culprit had apparently vanished. Most people thought that, with the improved trains and boats of the day, the crook might be anywhere. "Indeed," said Phileas Fogg, "it is now possible to go completely around the world in eighty days." Everyone thought that was impossible. Fogg bet half his fortune that he could make the journey around the world and return to his club at the stroke of noon, exactly eighty days later.

Fogg left immediately with his servant Passeportout. As soon as the two had left, the police began to suspect that Fogg had made the bet to get himself out of England. They thought that he himself was the robber they were seeking! Of course that was not true, but Fogg had no chance to clear himself. The dangers encountered by Fogg and Passeportout during the trip were many, for there were still many wild spots left in the world in those days.

Fogg and Passeportout took every form of transportation imaginable and made good time. But when Fogg arrived in London he was caught by the police. They held him a day past his deadline—or so he thought. He was sure that he had lost the bet, but Passeportout noticed the date on a newspaper and discovered they had arrived in London a day earlier than they thought they had. They had both forgotten that in traveling eastward they had crossed the international date line, gaining a day. Fogg rushed to the club and astonished the members by winning his wager with ten minutes to spare.

Help our travelers around the world. Keep away from the bloodthirsty desert chiefs, the fierce African warriors, the Indian braves on the warpath and the meddlesome London police.

Solutions

Cinderella, *page 2*

Jack and the Beanstalk, *page 6*

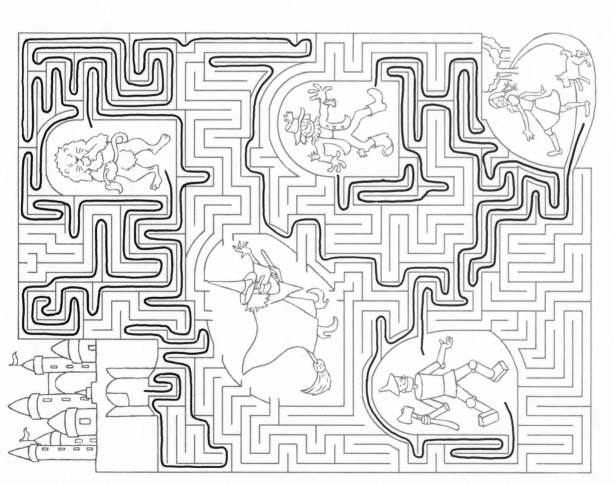

The Wizard of Oz, *page 4*

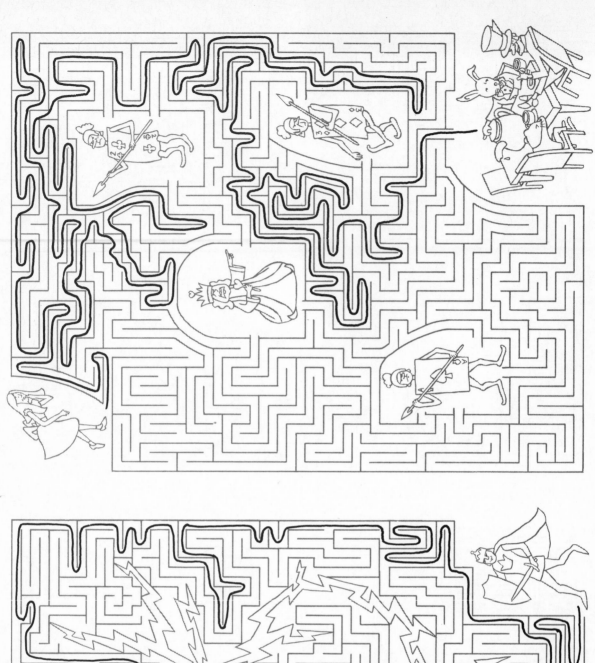

Alice's Adventures in Wonderland, *page 10*

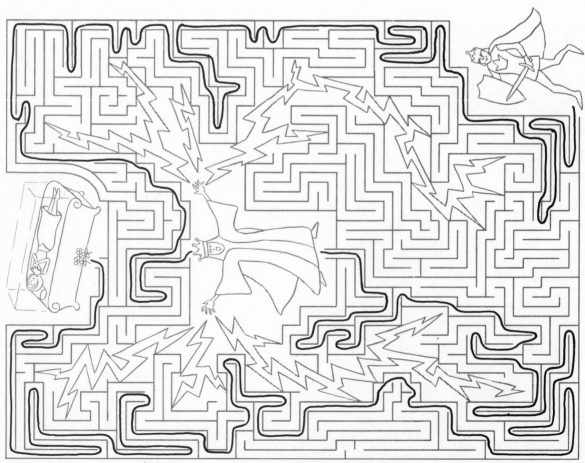

Snow White, *page 8*

50

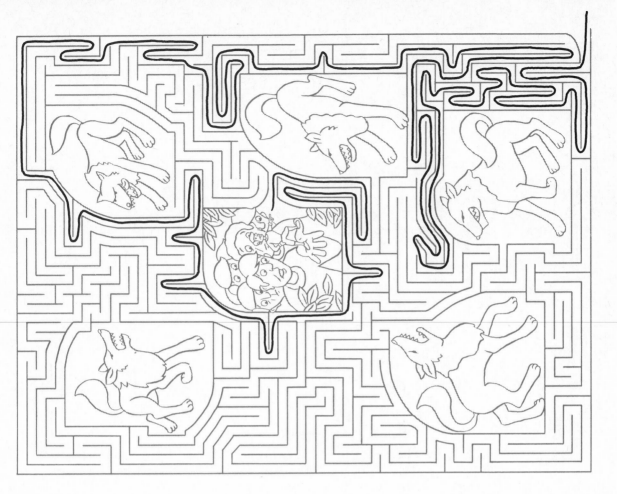

Little Tom Thumb, *page 14*

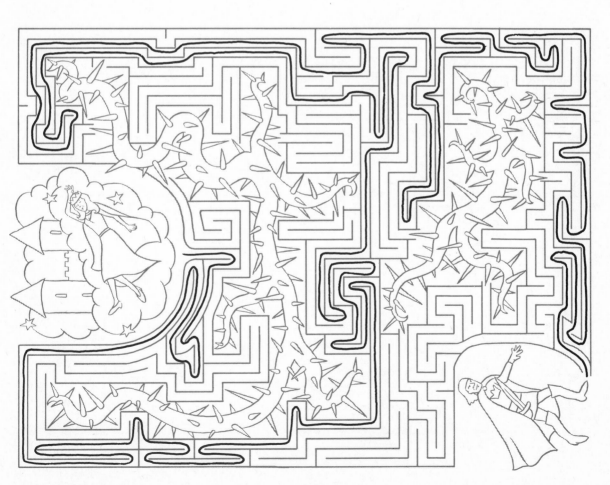

Sleeping Beauty, *page 12*

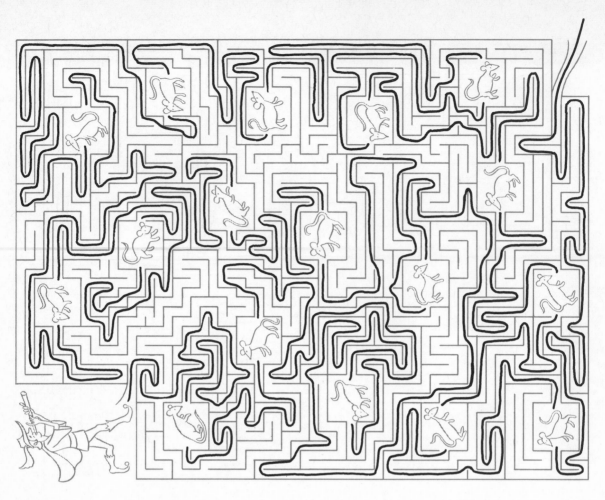

The Pied Piper of Hamelin, *page 18*

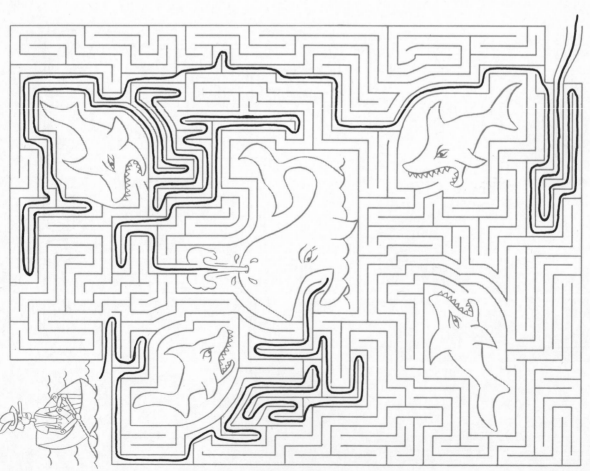

Pinocchio, *page 16*

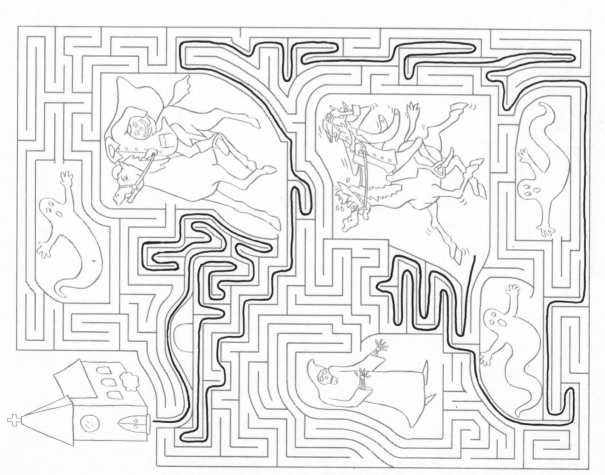

The Legend of Sleepy Hollow, *page 20*

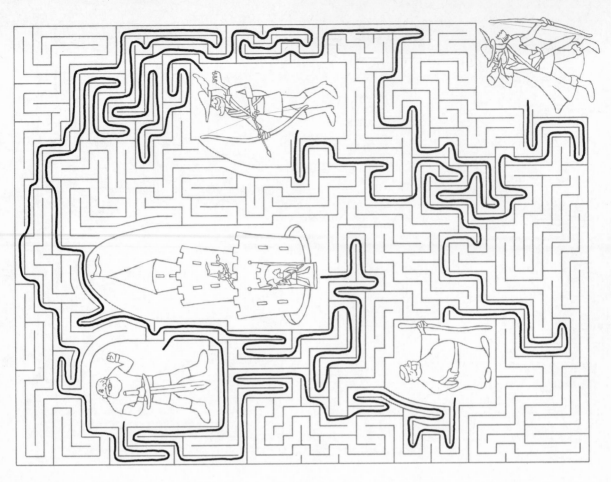

Robin Hood, *page 26*

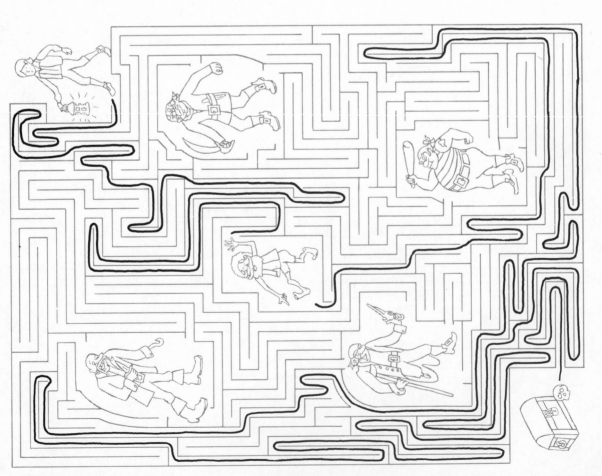

Treasure Island, *page 24*

Hercules, page 30

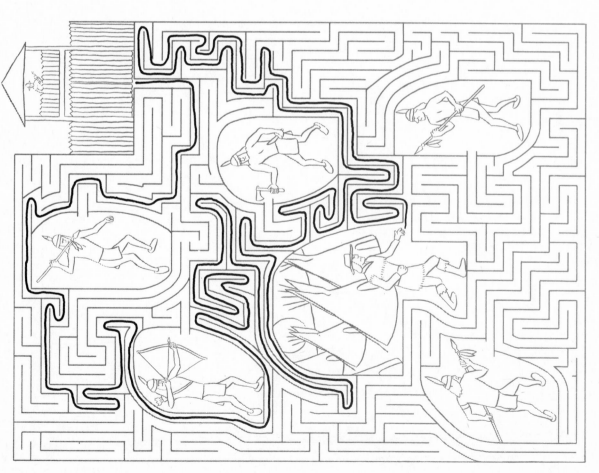

Daniel Boone, page 28

55

Jason and the Argonauts, *page 34*

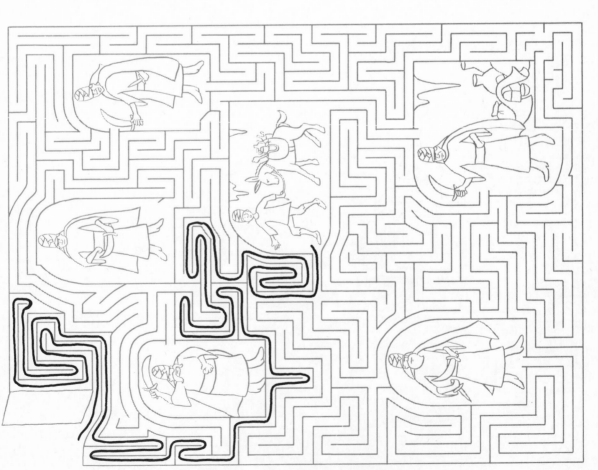

Ali Baba and the Forty Thieves, *page 32*

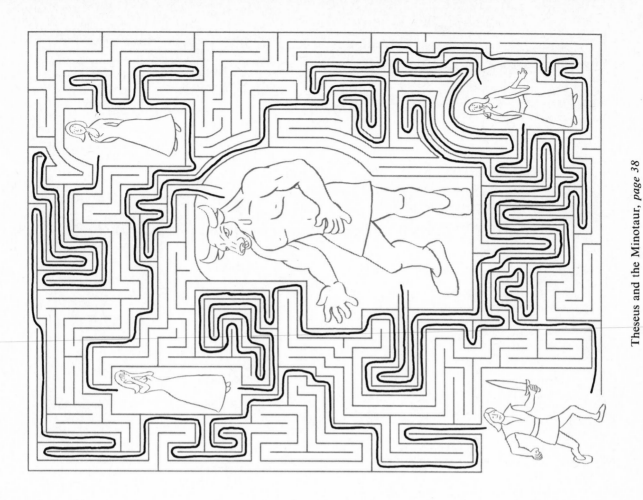

Theseus and the Minotaur, *page 38*

Aladdin and the Magic Lamp, *page 36*

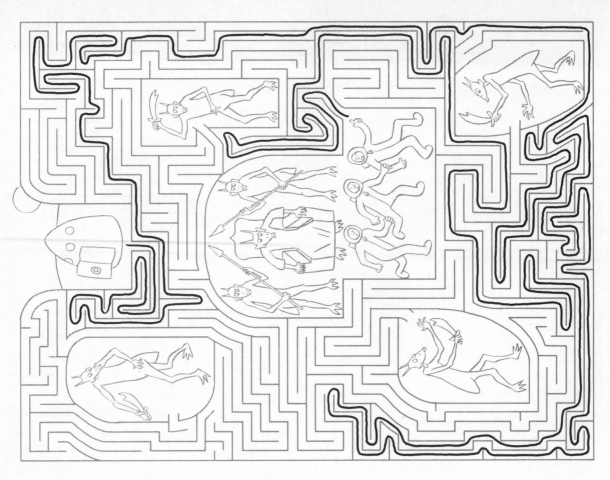

From the Earth to the Moon, *page 42*

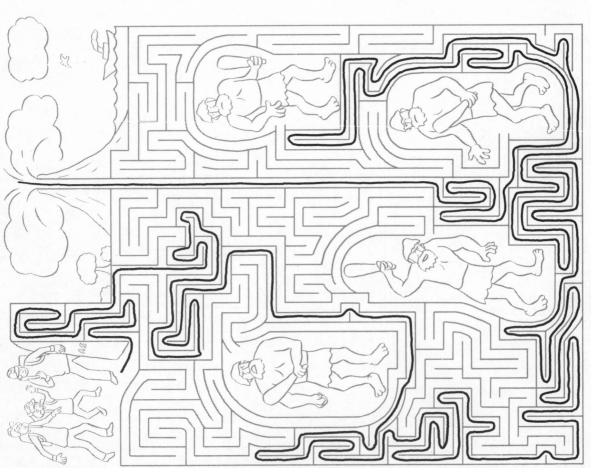

Journey to the Center of the Earth, *page 40*

Around the World in Eighty Days, *page 46*

Twenty Thousand Leagues Under the Sea, *page 44*